Dedication

For my Mother. Thank you for your unconditional love, guidance and wisdom. This book is dedicated to you Ma, and is a reflection of your faith and prayers. So rest now in knowing that the seed has indeed fallen on good soil.

I love you, Bubba

Forward

Sunday Dinner is a series of poems brought together to tell a story in which the author hopes to encourage renewed faith in the power of God. Follow along as the author takes you on a real life journey where although fear and doubt are a constant the mercy of God is always present.

Prologue
On a Sunday

Dear Mother,
on March 10th in 1940,
you were born
on a Sunday,

and although it may appear
to seem like a lifetime
you haven't been here in years
but to me
it seems like a lifetime

and these dreams,
are the only thing
that keep me
in my right mind.

Dear Mother,
I'm enduring this mourning
at best
and if your being sent
is the Lords gift
then I'll enjoy this courtship
with rest,

but if I should die

before I wake
please just allow me
to fly high,

cause I desire
to see her
more then anything
and Lord I know
I don't deserve these wings
but let Your will be done,

and I know that it might not
seem logical but
if You can light the earth
with the sun
then You can reunite her
with the son

through You
anything is possible
so I pray,

but I won't celebrate the day
cause it hurts,
Mom I mourn this day
cause it's the date
of your birth
reversed

and so I cry,
cause its hard
to have to say goodbye
on the same day
that you gave me life

Dear Mother,
on March 10th in 1974
I was born,
on a Sunday.

SUNDAY DINNER

Roderick Parchman

Part One
"Pray On It". ~ Momma

Chapter 1

"...That you may know the hope to which He has called you..."
Ephesians 1:18

The Prayer of the Prodigal Son

Lord Your callin'
is all in me now
all will see the meek serve

and I'm enthused
that You'd choose me
and I'm determined
to speak words

so use me
to be heard

and Your gospel will reach
as many as possible
and all will come
to seek Your face

that's why we praise
and honor You

just return Your son
to his rightful place

and Lord
forgive me
for being prodigal

Chapter 2

"Yea, though I walk through the valley of the shadow of death, I will fear no evil: for thou art with me; thy rod and thy staff they comfort me."
Psalms 23:4

Trials and Tribulations

Lord They told me when I seek You
I'd go through trials and tribulations,
but I was seeking You
to get me through

so now I'm hesitatin'
debatin'
should I continue to move forward Lord
in search of Your reward?

Cause I'm tired
I've cried
I've paid my tithes
but my lights ain't on no more

plus I'm laid off
so I done strayed off
of the beaten path
cause this path is beatin' my…

Ask and ye shall receive
is what they all tellin' me,
but I don't believe
cause I haven't received
and that's what y'all fail to see

So my trials and tribulations

start to cloud my meditation
now impatiently I'm waitin'
thinkin' Lord have You forsaken?

So the Prodigal Son
is back to square one,
with a pack of narcotics
a gun,
walkin' with swag
I'm cool like that
braggin' and lackin' none

cause I'm well paid now
walkin' a path the world laid down,
forgettin' the half
where You laid out on the cross
my debits paid out

Cause I thought it would be good
in the hood,
you know
fancy cars
in and out of bars
yeah
it was all good in the hood

But I never could'a seen this happenin',
a bullet ripped clean

through my abdomen,
I screamed for You Lord!
and fell to the floor
cause now I'm feelin' the wrath of men

but I got a praying Mother,
so I made it through that
without a colostomy bag
and now I'm believin'
You had my hand

and now I boldly stroll
this Holy road
and fall into the role of Job
and seek ye first
the Kingdom of gold
and submit to You my soul

and as I'm steppin'
into a New Testament,
I'm blessed to share my test
with men,

cause I realized that,
"He saw the best in me",
and that's why
He was testin' me.

Chapter 3

"I am the resurrection and the life. The one who believes in me will live, even though they die".

John 11:25-26

Death at the Door

Death was at the door
and I was scared

scared of the fact that my life
didn't reflect Yours Lord

I was givin less
cause I wanted more
at war in the flesh
and You didn't manifest Your glory

death had come for me
and I was scared

so I began to frantically search
for the nearest bible
though panicking
my plan to contend
with this fierce rival
or at least try to

cause my life was being cut short
like a hem
so I began stalling
recalling every hymn that I knew
which were few
cause I never truly knew Him

and I thought I was playing it safe
by straddling the fence
amazed with grace
but sadly convinced
that I was saved
when I really wasn't

instead of seeking first the kingdom
I sought these earthly riches
that now seem worthless

nervous in service
searching for worldly things
that serve no purpose
in Your kingdom

Lord I'm scared
to open the door
cause I might be facin damnation

so I'm placin myself
in a place of consecration
and I'm glad He's erasing past deeds
and racing pass me
setting a pace
so I can chase Him

but He lapped me,
now I'm being left behind
cause His will didn't align with mine

and I'm crying for forgiveness
blind to the signs
so I was declined at the entrance

now get this
I knew there'd probably be a time
when I'm supposed to be convicted
cause now someone is knocking
and it's not Jehovah's witness

death was at the door
and I was scared

Part Two
"You Gotta Run On And See What The End Gon Be."~ Momma

Chapter 4

"He is a liar and the father of lies."
John 8:44

In Fire

(Satan Speaks)
Today I saw your soul hurtin',
so much so that I saw me in you.
I'm certain.

So I'm encouraging you
to nourish this person—
to free yourself from this burden
would be worthless.

You need me.

Your heart is weak,
and you won't be able to sleep if you keep me.
I'm needy,
so kneeling won't be easy,
and my lease won't expire
until you desire
to pray without ceasing.

Yes, now my presence is increasing,
so there's no need for you to be blessed.
As long as I am your guest
you won't need anything.

So pray and have patience.
Praise Him through your tribulations—
I'm waitin'.

'Cause when prayers go unanswered
I become a cancer to the patient,
spreading,
infecting your spirit.

I'm the reason you experience pain
from which there'll be no deliverance.

So experiment.

'Cause not only will I cause you
suffering and misery,
but your affliction will be so intense
that you'll forget about His victory.

And the scriptures that they preach
won't measure up against me.

You see,
I am the enemy.

And my promises are obvious.
I can offer you a kingdom,
but you must refuse
to acknowledge His.

After all, He died,
and only that which is below
can actually rise.

So I offer you
these earthly presents once again.

I've been present since your birth,
which is why you were all born in sin.

So rejoice
in knowing that you've already made your choice,
yet you fail to realize—

'cause I dwell amongst you in disguise,
pacifying you with lies,
providing all that you desire.

And when you die,
it is I
who will baptize you
in fire.

Chapter 5

"Do not fear for I am with you"
Isaiah 41:10

But God!...

But God—is it too late? It can't be too late. My intentions were for repentance, but my decisions wouldn't allow me complete submission. And since nobody told me much about His grace being sufficient, I'm face to face with the Judge now, facin' a sentence. Then I admitted,

"I heard Your word, Lord—it wasn't in vain."

Then He replied,

"BUT YOU DENIED ME THRICE AND DIDN'T EXALT MY NAME."

ME: "Wait, I know, but if You show me where to walk, then I'll go."

GOD: "I GAVE YOU A MAP TO READ, A PLACE TO MEET, AND A PATH TO FOLLOW."

ME: "But give me a chance!"

GOD: "I GAVE YOU A LIFETIME TO BELIEVE IN MY WORD. YOU DIDN'T RECEIVE IT OR FEEL YOU NEEDED ME TIL PROBLEMS OCCURRED."

ME: "But I got these scriptures on my arm—Matthew, Mark, Luke, and John."

GOD: "SON, I WAS AIMING FOR YOUR HEART. YOU JUST MISREAD MY PSALMS AND YOUR HESITANCE TO GIVE ME REVERENCE…"

ME: "Lord, I meant to repent…"

GOD: "AND WHERE'S THE EVIDENCE? 'CAUSE I BROUGHT YOU THROUGH YOUR STRUGGLES AND HAVEN'T HEARD FROM YOU SINCE. I'VE WATCHED YOU ALL YOUR LIFE, SINCE YOU WERE FIRST CONCEIVED."

ME: "Then You know I've done some right. There's people worse than me. Plus, I've been baptized…"

GOD: "REALIZE YOU'VE ONLY WET YOUR SKIN, AND IT DOESN'T MEAN A THING IF YOU DON'T LET ME IN."

ME: "But I gave You praise…"

GOD: "IT WAS SELDOM, AND I WON'T STAY IF I'M NOT WELCOME. ON THIS DAY, YOU WILL SEE HELL…"

ME: "Son! of God, forgive me. I'm just not ready, and my soul, I know, is empty—but I'll change if You let me. I went astray during my youth, but now I offer my life."

GOD: "THERE'S NO EXCUSE WHEN I'M THE WAY, THE TRUTH, AND THE LIFE."

Then I screamed, "But God!"… but He was gone, like a thief in the night

Part Three
"Good God Almighty!"
~Momma

Chapter 6

"For many are called, but few are chosen."
Matthew 22:14

Kinda Christian

I'm what you would call kinda Christian
one who's mindful of the commitment
but I haven't quite committed
see I'm straddling the fence
battling against this calling
that's constantly calling
causing me to fall short of His glory

so I worry about going through various trials
cause I've yet to figure out
how to count it all joy

you see my thinking is this
as long as I repent
it's a given that I'm given mercy
He personally dispersed these perjures
and permanently removed my burdens
because He first loved me

so I guess I'm like Paul in a sense
in that I die daily
but I'm content in my condition
so I'm lacking the sense God gave me

and the crazy thing is
we're quick to sing praises
of how we honor and adore Him
then we use a facade
as if we can fool God
every Sunday morning

but this is why I'm torn within
cause I'm not quite sanctified yet
I'm dying to be born again
just like Frankenstein

so in their eyes
I'm supposedly a monster
who's posing as a Christian
when I know He sees imposters
which is why I don't even bother with a mask

but I'm dressed in my Sunday's best
for these Acts
and He knows that I'm playin' this role
man

and He bruised my soul
when He convicted me
but He didn't leave a Mark

and as long as I resist
the call from You Lord
I will always be Luke warm

cause first Peter denied Christ
so if you don't wanna be left
then you must choose right

because He gave us all free will
so it's time to make a decision

and as for me
I'd much rather live
then be kinda Christian

Chapter 7

"But when you ask, you must believe and not doubt, because the one who doubts is like a wave of the sea, blown and tossed by the wind."

James 1:6

Back of the Church

I sit,
in the back of the church,

because it seems that I wasn't deemed seasoned enough
to seize the season
that was set aside for the sanctified

so I'm,
in the back of the church,

wondering why my cries went unheard,
reeling inside feeling denied
even when I tried to apply the word,

searching the Holy Bible for a verse,
cursed with vitals
that a revival couldn't reverse,

if only shouting worked,
doubting the promise promised
these prophesies
that were probably not for me,
in the first place,

first grace eluded me
then prayers and praise excluded me
all because I sat in the back
tryin to snack off fruitless trees.

Cause it seems that,
my foundation wasn't built on solid rock,
so I'm bound to limitations
shrouded in impatience

pacing praying prayers
that lacked penetration,

and all the while I'm in the back
drowning in my frustration
cause patience is a virtue
that was reserved for the few
on the first pew

and I'm,
I'm in the back of the church

but it's not for lack of space
you see I'm contagious
so I can't embrace my neighbors

I'm afraid of the sanctified
and scared to appear faithless
and I'm faceless in this place

I misplace praise
I'm missin' grace,

my worship wasn't worth it
I'm misinterpreted as a Saint,

and I pray without conviction
somehow convinced
that I can change,

but He rose up from the grave
and now I know
that I've been saved,

and yet I remain…

in the back of the church.

Chapter 8

"For we walk by faith, not by sight."
Corinthians 5:7

It's Alright

My faith is being tested
to the fullest,
confessin' my need
for a blessin'

yet I'm sweatin' bullets
at the pulpit,
and although I'm unsure
about Your plans Lord
I'm raisin' my hands

they said His grace
would be enhanced
if I just praised Him
in advance
so I stand,
for the alter call

cause man,
I've faltered y'all,
but I probably wouldn't be lost
at all
if I could recall the laws
that were taught by Paul

cause see my flaws
were made clear,
and I'm aware
that He was sent here
and laid in the center,
of the cross
for my sins here

so when I pray
it's sincere,
Lord, it's alright,
right?

Cause I don't know sometimes,
and I'm not sure
if You noticed
when I was at my lowest,

but I'm tryin to stay focused
and my mind is stayed
on this word
cause I heard
if I knock
then He'd open,

so I'm hoping
it's alright
cause I'm still in my mess
but I'm trying to be still
til Your will manifest

and yet,
these problems still bother me
and it became obvious to me
that I wasnt livin'
according to Your policy

but its alright,
cause theres alot
that He's promised me
and I believe
in all honesty
that He's not forgotten me

so its alright,
its alright,
Lord, its alright,
right?

"...and lo I'am with you always, even unto the end of the world." Amen.
Matthew 28:20

Epilogue

Sunday Dinner

My Mother made dinner
every Sunday,

and I remember
just like yesterday,
coming in to hear her humming hymns
and asking
if we wanted a plate.

But make no mistake
cause even though we were allowed to self serve
it was her selfless ways
and because of her faith
she allowed herself to serve

and so she would serve,
that's how she made sure
that every plate got filled
so I wouldn't leave the table
until I ate my fill.

Cause it was more then enough
plus the aroma from the food
always filled the room up
and I could tell
by the smell coming from the pots
what she stirred inside.

But it was worth the wait
when my stomach was in knots
like something stirring inside
every Sunday
as soon as she came home from church.

But she wouldn't rest
until the table was blessed.
She gave the Lord praise first.

But now I search
for what was lost to me
cause it was more than just a meal.
It was her dressin'
dressed in blessings
and I feel her presence still.

So when she bowed
and said grace
it was by grace
I'm convinced.

It's why my Mother died
on a Sunday
and we haven't had Sunday dinner,
since.

Acknowledgements

First, I thank God—for His grace, His mercy, and for giving me the means to be a blessing while glorifying His name.

My parents, Willard and Geneva Parchman—though both have gone on to glory—left us with a strong spiritual foundation, where even in the hardest times we learn to call on the name above every other name.

Jamal and Sonia Gaines for maintaining the gift of family and togetherness, and for allowing me to see that this tradition still exists.

I also want to thank the lifelong friends of my parents who stepped in to fill certain roles that where left in their absence.

Apostal Charles King II and his wife Emma King for the prayer and support. Who no matter how old I get will always call me "Bubba".

Thank you for your warm smiles and open arms and for helping me on this journey. Beverly Bush (my Mothers gift to us.) After Mom passed you fed my brothers and me like you were feeding an army! And those rolls…good God Almighty!!

I just thank you for your love, guidance and countless hours of counsel and most of all, for always offering us a warm invitation to Sunday Dinner.

About Sunday Dinner

Sunday Dinner represents unconditional love and service—two traits that defined the walk of Christ. More than a meal, it is a tradition rooted in love and togetherness that, along with the elders, is slowly fading away. With them go guidance, wisdom, prayer, and the kind of knowledge only lived experience can give. Yet what they poured into us remains, calling us to keep the table, carry the lessons, and pass on what once fed both body and soul.

This is why Sunday dinner matters. It was never just about eating—it was about being fed.

"One generation shall praise Thy works to another."

Psalm 145:4

About the Author

Roderick Parchman is a spoken word artist born in South Bend, Indiana, where he was raised in the church. Some of his earliest memories are waking on Sunday mornings to the hum of gospel music calling the house to worship. He began performing his poetry at church functions, sharing stories of faith through spoken word. His Mother, his greatest supporter, encouraged him to take his words further and ultimately inspired him to write this book. Sunday Dinner is dedicated to her.

"God gave me an assignment in the midst of my pain that kept me."

~RJP

www.ingramcontent.com/pod-product-compliance
Lightning Source LLC
Chambersburg PA
CBHW051337150726
47997CB00004B/1503